Excursive

Excursive
Essays [Partial & Incomplete]

(on Abstraction, Entity, Experience, Impression,
Oddity, Utterance, &c.)

Elizabeth Robinson

ROOF BOOKS
New York

ISBN: 978-1-931824-76-7
Library of Congress Control Number: 2022951879

Book design by Deborah Thomas.

Acknowledgments: My thanks to the editors and presses who have pub-
lished poems from this collection: *Ambush, Another Chicago
Magazine, Clade Song, Columbia Poetry Review, Black Warrior Review,
Bombay Gin, Boog City, Brooklyn Rail, Conjunctions, Dear Navigator,
Eight by Eight, Eleven Eleven, Eoagh, Fence, Free Verse, Hambone,
Horse Less Review, Jubilat, Letter Box, LVNG, Noon, Occasional
Religion, The Recluse, Peep Show, Seventeen Seconds, Skidrow
Penthouse, Summer Stock, The Offending Adam, Touch the Donkey,
Typo, Verse Daily, Volt,* and *White Wall Review.*

I thank the editors of the following for publishing chapbooks
including material from this manuscript: *A Tangle in Every Instance*,
published by Sara Lefsyk for Ethel Press, *Under Necessity of Wind*
published by Woodland Pattern for tinder/tender press, and *Three Ef-
forts at Arrival and a Series of Departure* published by Valerie Coulton
for Palabrosa.

NEW YORK | Council on   This book is made possible, in part, by the New York
STATE OF | the Arts   State Council on the Arts with the support
OPPORTUNITY.
of the Office of the Governor and the New York State Legislature.

Roof Books   Roof Books
are published by Segue Foundation   are distributed by
300 Bowery Fl 2   Small Press Distribution
New York, NY 10012   1341 Seventh Street
seguefoundation.com   Berkeley, CA. 94710-1403
                                    800-869-7553 or spdbooks.org

For Randy

Table of Contents

On the Apparent

"World" does not mean "harm."

"Body" does not mean "straight," but

it has lost its curve.

Body cries at the loss of the curve,

the roundness of ass that

made "world" a place to sit

in comfort. The fleshy indent

at the waist that helps Body

turn in sleep. "Here" does not

mean "wrong." "O" does not

mean "I exclaim." "Mouth"

does not open at the cry. "World"

would be "mouth" that has lost

its curve. "Mouth," "O," gentle

rigidity. "World" lost in

the saying, not saying.

"Lip" a gesture that

presses against "lip."

On Beauty

Like anything of import, it is invisible. Like "god."

A small child wakes in the middle of the night having

had an orgasm. Inexplicable.

She attributes this to "god."

Would beauty, then, be a form of innocence?

Somewhere in the dark of the house, the heat rumbles on.
Radiator.

Wordlessly, from inside her mind, the child tells "god" that if one
closes one's eyes long enough,

one sees it, the cobalt at the center, suffusing an edge of
light green. Rippling.

Rippling outward from where she hovers above it.

On Bitterness

Consider this, that all

sensation may be sectioned like citrus.

The membrane (what holds sensation in)

is the bitter part.

Therefore this poem will proceed in sections.

*

Section one,
having to do with bitterness and perversity

When young, the two girls sat side by side in church.

The taller one, the one with the long curly hair, chewed
mercilessly on her nails.

The buck-toothed girl looked on.

The mother of the taller procured a bottle of bitter liquid,
and this she painted on her daughter's ragged nails to deter
her chewing.

Whereupon the buck-toothed girl demanded that her nails be
painted too.

The two girls sat side by side in the pew avidly sucking the
bitterness from their fingers.

*

We renege on the plan of sections.

This is all the bitterness we can portray today.

On the table, the white pith broadcasts its spotlessness.

The very needle of acrimony brightens so as to be

threaded through with the filaments of this—remainder

of fruit.

On Boredom

Wasn't it flawless?

Out of the corner of the eye, our condition appeared stable. It

didn't refract into different colors.

    Every day diligent to the day's variegation, always

        treading on the blotches, scratching snot where it's
            dried on the sleeve.

    Counting the syllables in "every" every day.

Until by mistake

the day had no error to pursue.

It tugged on the so-scrubbed hands and left them bland
with perfection.

It licked the face and left no residue.

On the Bride and Her Dead Flowers

It was hard to remember how they smelled originally, if they had
the fragrance

of the hothouse or the garden.

But one should start with the hardest part first.

Like saying, "I want a divorce" to a person who shrugs and walks away.

As in

trying to remember what is the hardest part.

The bouquet preserved intact because the bride,

as instructed, hung it upside down. Docility.

They had the fragrance of.

They had the fragrance of what memory does with indifference.

The most difficult part—oh, that.

On Cancer

First you die, and then you are merely chronic.
First you do this, and then you do that.
First you love narratives and then they all become redundant
and develop a stale body odor. Firstly, you reach into your gut
and then scatter the jewels you pull from that magical site.
First you are a saint and then you are just dead. First you are
a thread and then you are an appalling braid. Look at the
sapphires, carnelians, diamonds that mingle with the second
term, the *then*. Then you have looked. Then you are the culprit.
Then you must eat raw vegetables. Then there is no penitence
good enough. First you were bad, and then you were not good
enough. First, in dying, you desert everyone who ever loved
you and then they are forced to make a scholarship in your
name. Then you have died and the first recipient turns her
seraphic eyes toward you and they are made of diamonds.
Because winning is the hardest hard, the jewel that can be cut
only by itself. Your gut is now gone, and you reach into other
organs. You find generic glitterings there, replacements at more
affordable cost.

On Being Changed and Unchanged

We are uncertain how to pronounce "Kamala" and "Chesa Boudin."
This does not change.

We are unchanged in recognizing that a poem is mostly a list.
We change its lyric to the rhythm of our grievances.

We have changed our pronouns or
they remain unchanged, but now we list them,
adjunct to our names.

We continue, as always, to get our vaccinations,
but now we are inoculated with alternative facts.

We have, at least some of us, changed, have pulled up
the green turf
we once called "lawn" and planted weedy, drought-resistant plants.

Our neighbor, who washes each of his cars on a different day
of the week, is unchanged, hose in hand.

The sidewalk is immutable and yet achy with the steam
that rises from its saturated plane.

We change without intending to, now less hair in the armpit,
a pair of reading glasses, a new address, but maintain
that we are the same person we've always been.

We are unchanged in being oblivious to our frailties
until they change us irremediably.

We continue to send text messages, but
our children, wincing at the abruptions of the world,
have changed us, removing our punctuation
which they find so harsh

On Conspiracy

Doubt is the most
delicious thing
a body can know. As if
to have a swath
of velvet wrapped
around one's
bare shoulders
and the feel
of anonymous
fingers hand-
feeding morsels
of sweet,
potentially toxic,
oh, if
only, a body likes
its dangers to be
safe, like,
say, having sex
with a cousin,
but really just
pressing two
sweaty pre-
pubescent
chests
together in
the August
humidity before
running back
to kick the
can, you know—
some games
are like that
and don't we
all like them, I

know you do,
you too, we know
suspicion is
erotic, but as the
world unspools
around us,
facts
are not even
erotic-adjacent
and you
know what else
we like—the texture,
the nap of the
fraying world
between our toes
as we walk over
the debris and blame
them, the perpetrators,
for every
nefarious act,
what they
want to take
away from us, the
shocking,
shocking things
they did and, best
yet, what they
want to do to
us, to you and
me, tied
up in so many
knots of tangled
world, flesh
bulging pinkly
between the bindings,
and don't you love
that our safe word

is "safe"
because, you
know, you have
to trick them, the
way they say
the opposite
of what they mean,
you have to insist
on the opposite
of that, like the
woman whose
lover once whispered
to her when they
were at the bar sipping
a glass of wine, that
her breast had slipped
out of her low-cut
dress and that her nipple
was showing, so
she laughed and
slapped his cheek,
aware that he
was lying, I mean
she never doubted
that she was meant
to doubt him, until
later she looked up
at a mirror and saw
her naked breast, and
how she shivered
in pleasure, how she's
never been able
to trust him since.

On Contentment

One long hank of hair

potentially silky, potentially dull,

potentially mind, potentially body, and

the teeth of the comb

tugged, separating strand by

strand, yes, as the teeth of the comb

mark each filament, none different

from any other, parallel,

raking the endless, lank

tress of hair. Contentment combing

itself out. Contentment

more thorough than beauty, a soft

and felted snarl pulled from the comb,

a lock more curly than perfection, and potentially better.

On Cups

in memory of Michael Gizzi

This is a series of verses.

They stack like the vertebra, delicate

and susceptible to pain.

The cups are scattered on the mattress where the

dead man sleeps.

Each verse has its own prosody. Each says
"no."

A tower, like the vertebra, like a text
toppling over itself: flimsy cups piled up

and toppling.

Their harmonies say "no."

Peel off the bedding, why don't you. The monosyllabic

clink
of cups. As a cup is a memento. Dried

to its inner curve, a route, the spine of the tongue,

the modest decoration that makes it watertight.

On Depression

In the word "you" we see evidence
of geological depression.

The "y" dips down, a sharp valley.
The "o" refuses to receive.
The "u" is a cup of some depth.

The landscape in dismay spits
into the cup. The landscape

had harbored an undisclosed
but still evident

love for *you*.

It does not want to claim itself
as a swimmer drowning in the cup,
in the pool into which

it had spit. Who is
this landscape that falls

and always falls
into *you*—the body snagged

in the valley's cramp, the
flailing arms

of the maladroit swimmer
in the cup you

would drink from if
it were not *you*.

*

O to bay at a moon
that surpasses the landscape by

being other than a moon, an orb
that *you* may choose

to puncture. The landscape
rubs a dirty paw
on the eroded site

of its focus. Someone
poured the cup

of its contents, a landscape
drained on the landscape where saliva

still clings to the interior of the cup.

*

The sharp declivity of the valley

hints at a compensatory

proclivity for a peak. No such

formation in *you*, but the landscape

might forgive this by raising the

plane of depressions into the

emphasis which swallows the air

surrounding the hole

which once cupped it. Here: the clinging

moisture the landscape

pours out to measure contour—

a dust devil, a whirlpool cupping

its current.

On Editing

Editing was the perfect recursive process—

to return to the thing and make it more itself.

As a child, she enjoyed the idea that she could think a thought

while thinking of herself thinking it, a predisposition

toward editing which understands it as

uncanny oversight on

immediacy to thought. But never

was she able to be certain that she had actually

thought the thought while thinking of herself

thinking it.

To do this again and again, to strive for mastery

over the iteration that makes it pure.

Editing was never perfect, but it strove for purity:

recursiveness by excision. She edited and

she edited until it was possible

not that she thought, or thought herself into a thought

but that a thought existed, claimed

its site so that the mind could recur to it.

On the Electrical Circuit

It is a chase game.

The monkey chases the weasel.

Clockwise.

Counterclockwise.

The coil on the stove turns red.

A pattern of heat and infinity so seductive

that the child must lay her hand on it.

The circuit turns amorously complete—as the pattern

of a scar that marks something other than rupture—as

the hand melted to its continuity.

On Email

The way the wrist aches in its lazy lean

onto the keyboard

and, really, the way the message encrypts the

silence one sits in, unbodied—encrypts deadness

as dropped letter, incorrect address, the

attachment that one never remembers to attach.

A message swathed in a snarl of

distraction, spam, the body softening into

vacancy. Drafts that reveal a reply from

a dead friend. "Compose" is the icon

one clicks to begin, and yet how decompose

in the privacy of this silence? Here, where one can

pick one's teeth, thoughtfully comb the knots

from one's hair with one's fingers, send a message

that has nothing in its subject line. Always softly

evading circuits, always one's evasion of presence

a most vague and pleasing feature of one's

abstracted, raveled discomposure.

On Epiphanies

Old page so brittle it crumbles at the touch, old
flannel page.

Light shadows on the wall that make
the wall appear
streaked with rain.

(Just the fragments of rain, how they make
revelation, and not

the whole of water.) (And not
rain at all but light falling willy-
nilly through
blinds.) (Not the whole
of light, but a remainder of it.)

The page resolves to dust. Epiphany as what
cannot be saved.
Epiphany. Not revelation, but a release of scent.

Not fulfillment, but the aftertaste of it.
A sweetness that's slightly overripe.

On the Equinox

A sheep in a dream

dreamed the equinox

was a salt lick.

Its tongue was the sun

while the salt of the equinox

deposited itself on the equator.

Thus a dream is equal. Holding even

its night and its day. What all known living creatures

need in small amounts. Salt. A tongue that absorbs the dream's saliva.

A sheep pulls its wool from the dream to the real world, disturbing

the dream's parsing of

opposites. Which upsets the wool and salt,

all the whiteness that waited on itself.

This lost equilibrium of

discovery just before it evaporated

onto tongue or time.

On a Version of Eros

for Truong Tran

We make beautiful things from pornography.
The Venn diagram of eros is a colored moth
that lofts over two (or more) bodies
joining. Conjoining, pornography
is a crossword puzzle of
orifices. Only certain words
fit in their cavities. Only
certain fragments fit. Look
at diagram A. The fragmentary
genitalia: the palimpsest. There
are standby words that appear in virtually
every crossword puzzle and words
that, forbidden, appear in none. The moth
has infinitesimally small
reproductive organs. Its wings are
completely transparent, except when
they overlap with themselves. Who lights
on diagram B and shudders.

On Extinction

To theorize how to disclose what no longer exists.

To be
the Spix Macaw, Baiji, the Quagga, the Splendid Poison
Frog.

Or to be not.

To wonder whether a name is a proper noun or a marker
of cessation.

To capitalize anyway.

To discover it as a result of its passing.

To speak of the loss only by introducing it with an infinitive.

To sorrow without inflection.

To conjure the verb without binding it to subject or tense.

On Extinctions

Bucardo

I was a gently curving horn,

was agile,

drew myself to heights.

I dwindled.

I survived.

Thus, a tree grew and the tree collapsed

and I became a preposition to the collapse:

beneath.

A remainder of fur.

A hoof.

Wilderness little different than insemination.

I was an egg hollowed of its contents

and replaced by myself.

Replica mimicking extinction.

I was a lung, a hardening lobe, while

the moving air curved as though an ivory horn

and lay still.

On Extinctions

Tasmanian Tiger

Hope's keen nose smells itself. A muzzle
chewing at its own groin.

Undisturbed by visibility
since these many years.

If a creature
can be a site, a space—unoccupied
space.

Hope resists taxonomy—resists
the specimen photograph. Its distinctives

should remain indistinct else
extinct. Stripes on its haunches.

A presence resorbed to its own
abdominal pouch. Gestating absence.

Hope believes that what doesn't exist
never did.

A rigid tail
trailing out behind the not-it.

Straying as in.
As in stray.

Hope's pelt fitted tight to its hips, a presence
that stands in for the original.

To figure hope as a presence no one can verify.

On Fame

A departure from the self into its plural.

Doubt and aporia. I think.

An adolescent girl with perpetually mussed
hair who likes the body of a football player

from afar.

Fame is afar-ness
fantasized as nearness.

She goes to the football game but has no idea
how the game is played, cannot

from this distance

recognize the player whose ass

looked so good; they all look good.

She thinks so. Maybe. Or

maybe the cheerleaders, and their
bare, smooth legs shaved glossy

and without razor burn.

I don't know. Could she have been me,
sucking on a loose strand of hair?

The relative, vanishing fame of peers.
I am distracted by

the stadium lights,

how they make day out of night. One
of us stares unblinking at their glare

until our eyes water.

On Fashion

Fashion was a pause in nakedness.
Is a pause. Was.

Fashion is always temporal.

Cloud shirred across the bare waist of the sky.
Skin's ephemeral skin.

Fashion's silk cut on
flame's bias, stitched in ash.

Fashion tailors restless meteorology. Ruching the
dishabille before it recognizes it has a body. A storm.

Fashion is the orifice of the garment slipped over
undisclosed cavity.

Waterhole, leghole, firepit, collar, mine, seam, nest,
cloche, cave, buttonhole, bra cup, well, air blousing
around invisible gasses, glove, even abyss.

Fur of no living thing, tide pleating itself, aftermath
that originates the color of day's end.

Fashion is a form outgrown, a thing bigger than
its own size. Fashion's fattened nudity tattooed

with madder and indigo. Fashion's
crisis of environment and confidence—

time, time again. A gauze that
hesitates, yes, pauses, a shawl

dissolving on the shoulder of the wind.

Fog

Soft, tidal. One had no need to decide

whether to trust it. It recurs.

It told us

about skin. How skin

is a form of sleep, visible from no measurable

distance. Yes, skin

reassured us.

Coming closer.

Drowse wrapping its leg

and skin into the burr

of sweat, curl.

Yes, a cloud that stole by us as we implored it for sleep, asked it

(who trusts us and us

not trusting it) to put our pelt

back on our spines, our buttocks,

on the tails that corkscrew into the atmosphere.

Gerrymandering

Define boundary if you can.
As if a boundary were a district (from the Latin
for *distringere*, to "draw apart"). So

draw it:

District in the shape of
the blue jay's ominous arrival
at the birdfeeder, in the shape
of the crippled stumps of a pollarded
tree, in the shape of the voices that
arise from over the fence from
men leaning against a car in the
sunshine discussing Barry Bonds
and smoking weed, in the shape of
a top-heavy child on a pogo stick, in

the shape of In God We Trust.

To draw asunder, compel, distrain.

In the shape of Harold of
the purple crayon, drawing a
bed and drawing up the

covers, a drawstring
pulled tight, a purple
garotte, some would say,
in the shape of a necklace.

On Getaways

This is the destination.

Ardent body of the beloved approaching

is our getaway. Haven is not adequate.

Herein is in here. This is the way out.

*

In the tale of the glamorous criminal,

there is sex and there is the getaway car.

Technically, this is not correct. But herein,

my correction:

slick surface. The getaway

is surface. It is brightly lacquered color.

But it is grievously distressed. No getaway

attaches to the pictorial. To the humiliation

of the literal. Get away—

surface unattached to its route.

*

Getaway kiss.

Do you recollect our kiss. In the dark,

a hand on a breast, a city street, a tongue

in the throat, in the speaker's throat,

in a column of sound, in a column of slick

surface sounding,

sounding off,

engine revving in the blank of the speaker's

throat, guillotine

slicing through the rush

of the kiss in its

vacuum.

*

Oh Bonnie, oh Clyde

do not look upon us as poseurs. Our love

was more sincere than yours. Though

we stole nothing we could name, our thefts were as intentional

as yours. Bright lacquer, I change my pronoun

from singular to plural so that I may have a lover.

So that my guilt may be true. So that the solitude

of my desire for escape can attach from surface to

desire for a surface.

*

What then is a culprit?

Herein my confession. The blather

of celebrated guilt. I want the beloved's

body as I want nothing else. As proof.

I remember what cannot

be remembered otherwise, and hence my moral turpitude.

The bars of the cell make a pattern that lacks true depth.

*

Guillotine or paper cut:
not a trivial equation. Both

so efficient. Both, like the revving engine,

cutting the roadway
into lanes.

*

I only wanted to stop being

there.

Certainly I used the terms of legal discourse:
I offered a

gloss.

Summary judgment.

The slick surface bounced an image off itself

as though (derisive)

this were escape.

I forgot the point of origination, therefore

how could I mark progress

away from it?

*

A last word on the lover, the missing document,
the conventions of

the road.

All that

did kiss:

Our surpassing

conviction

was the smack of sound

when surface meets surface or

is torn asunder

from it.

      (As in the dark, all cats are gray,

         so in the realm of getaways, all roads lead astray.)

                  *

Herein my destination:

a manifest desire to abandon this text

for any

other.

The getaway was not successful.

The lips are two shining surfaces.

The mouth is a single uniform surface unable

to kiss.

It is sliced via papercut

into two lanes.

The speaker's lips part, who says nothing,

famed, defamed,

the engine of the surface rolling over itself. Oh, lover

darken the road; the cul-de-sac that intention subscribes to,

like a lamp throwing sheen on a rain-stricken street. Like,

but not self-same. Likeness

its cruel captivity.

On Getting the Dog to Eat

7 a.m.
The dry food in the bowl, the medication in its chewy pocket,
some wet food smeared on top.

She does not eat.

A garnish of leftover fortune cookie crushed on top.

She does not eat.

We leave for work.

I return in the afternoon.

She rushes to the fetid bowl of food and eyes me.
She eats it all.

She goes outside and shits.

Having shit, she wanders a loop away
and then back to
the excrement. To sniff it.

Invariable pattern.

This is dog mind: we are manifest not because of what we are but
because of what we emit.

We eat only to shit and, shitting, prove that we exist.

On the Good

What is the Good—

often considered irrelevant,

inexpedient (see: Bad).

       (But might we

permit a moment of

       tender possibility here?)

The good is a series of variables

that attach to no specific referents.

In other words—

       Yes, exactly. Other words. Ad infinitum.

       *

(We do permit

the salt its savor.

We care so little—no,

not so little, so

irrelevantly—

whose tongue it alights on.)

*

A further example:

the creature rushes excitedly to the door

at the arrival of its master or mistress.

It yelps, it weeps.

Its pleasure is so hard to read, an arrangement, a series of variables

so constellated (Are they good?)

which might otherwise suggest terror.

Yes, the good in relation to arrivals.

To be elaborated later.

If ever.

*

Here we find the good to be incorrigibly tardy.

This is the eros of goodness, the

delayed arrival.

Arrival is planted within another arrival.

*

The good—let us try this out—
can we make our model particular and concrete?

Let us say that the good is the art of scent.

Variables, then:
particulate matter, motes far too fine for the eye to see,
for the fingers to perceive

inside

the swath of airs through which they wash.

Here in the world pervaded by perfume, the breath

congests. Good is a delay,

breath obstructing the way of perfume.

On Gun

Gun was a noxious fume of impotence whether you wanted
gun or rejected gun.

Gun a plane flying at such distance that it appears to be silent.
Gun not silent. Insolent.

Gun the fur on a creature—
Gun for a facsimile trophy,
gun atrophy, unreal pelt,
gun molting.

Gun to church, to school, to party. Gunning, gunning, gunning gone.

Gun toddler wandering in gun-orphaned crowd.

Gun lobby where gun picks up its nametag for the conference.
Gun conferring, gun permitting.

Gun gargling, gun drowning its sorrows at X rounds per minute.
Gun bellying up to the bar or barrel: gun happy hour.
Hors d'oeuvres gun devours.

Gun courts court.
Gun legitimates concealed gun carry in New Gun City.

Gun conspiracy contrails are actual gun chemtrails.

Gun plane crashing ungun silent and ungun distant. Undeterred.
Gun's gun detritus engulfing the field.

Gun ventriloquist senator speaking gun lisp. Gun denture.
Gun gumming.
Gun god dialect damned gun.

Gun's stink conspiring, gun's bright tiny fuses in
gun hair-trigger of the gun's golden—no, gilt—
no, glittered—citizen nostrils.

On Happiness

*This essay lacks a topic sentence.

*It is looped like a jump rope over the back of a chair.

Your task is to enact an associative link

that will satisfy the demands of these

two

facts.

Because the elation of facts

tends not to last long.

On Heaven

Heaven is personal, a score to be settled:

You would recline on the divine and fluffy bed

if only to relish the bitter post-nasal

drip that burns down your throat.

Say it. Everything you spat out in the one life,

say again here. Cloud borne.

Heaven is a perfect parallel, no, a continuity

with all the antique rage, and if only

more eloquent. But no. You wake mute

and therefore perfected. God is your mattress.

You wake without a word more of it, your hair

tangled, a brittle stain burned through the counterpane

by the acrid stuff that had dripped from

your throat. And your eyes

still unfocussed with sleep.

On the Impossible

in memory of Colleen Lookingbill

Our encounters with daily life made it impossible
to know what the impossible was.

Say, a feature of the improbable in which breathing itself
was no longer necessary.

A beehive grew on the lung.

The impossible was a dire irritant. It revised itself incessantly; it
seduced the possible.

Meanwhile, there was honey coating every inhalation.

A sound of the industrious in place of the lung, the habitation

that exiled breath from possibility.

On Insomnia

Sleep drills a burr hole
in the head and comes in, conforming
itself to
the inside of the skull
except when
it fails to do that.
When was it you
kissed my right nipple,
then, Sleep, my left?
I was a Mint Morpho
pinned to antique wallpaper.
Or a hip, I dreamed,
luxuriating in
gravity amid summer grass.
Nocturnal breath clotting the burr hole.
How, Sleep, do you flip the page to
continue to write, right
to left, top, is it, to bottom?
I was a katydid paint-by-number somehow
stenciled on the verso.
Will you recognize what, Sleep,
I need you, species by species,
to recognize?
Feelers, mouth parts (Sleep)
Kisses to my right nipple
cause my back to arch like
an insect with its own sentience
whereupon you enter
the curve, Sleep, cinching me to
you like a girdle.

Left, left.

On Inundation

All arrivals are rumored.

Your lover has never been introduced by any name.
Your lover self-corrects, made of betrayal and then surfeit.

Made of too-muchness, of a current made of itself.
Made of something that responds to tide, is not tide.

Your lover sweeps down a hillside, all aftermath.
All sand, old rope, mulch.

This one who springs from the site that you thought had no spring.

All arrival: all impassable roads.

The lover was always one who had no antecedents and yet

whose progeny grind and rush in the ear.

Where the deluge is a fixation. Obsessive list of detritus.

Where your lover was something that saved itself, saved up
itself, a reservoir that battered

against the border until it gave itself away.

On Invocation

for Sandra Simonds

To invoke creates its own delay—

> as when the author denies herself the right to shower
> or even use the toilet

> (speaking hypothetically)

until she has completed some distasteful task.

Seen this way, denial or withholding is the form of invocation
par excellence.

But then, the act of showering turns out to be so onerous.

Afterward, one has to select and put on one's clothes, and
dressing itself is sometimes an act of invocation to the world

too difficult to take on.

*

The poet wonders if invocation is therefore the craft of delayed
gratification.

"Eat your creamed mushrooms before you get any dessert."

and later:

"You can't leave the table until you finish your mushrooms."

and much, much later:

The child sits in the shadowy dining room, alone
with a gelatinous mess of mushrooms chilling on her plate.

"Just go to bed."

*

Is the process of making a poem an invocation to
the self, or invocation to, after a fashion,
giving birth?

And isn't mothering's art of teaching delayed gratification in fact

a grand and prolonged practice of delayed gratification?

*

Or. The phenomenon of slamming one's fingers in the door:

pain that requires a body to jump up and down and just

live through it.

But as the body inclines forward over its pain,

what is it living *toward*?

*

Luckily, the author keeps a 1967
Random House Dictionary of the English Language
beside her desk,

Thus to invoke:

to call
to call for with earnest desire

to appeal to, as for confirmation
the magic formula used to conjure up a spirit

*

To insist: all of this fits, obscurely, together.

That is the nature of calling out.

That is the nature of addressing this language to a person
whom the author has met only once in the crowded entry of a
bookstore, and that only for a few moments.

This is the nature of the holding it in which, as we have already
established, is the very truth of calling out.

That is: the nature of one author addressing another.

*

Another example seems apropos.

History records the incident of a younger child biting his older
sibling.

("He's a flesh-eater," his uncle remarked.)

The child's preschool teacher suggested that for a pre-verbal
child, biting is one way that frustration gets exteriorized.

Think about it: to bite another, to take a piece of their self into
one's mouth when one is not yet able to speak—

well, isn't that to invoke speech of a different order?
Isn't that also to cause the aforementioned invocational pain,
pain that must simply be lived through?

*

Admit it:
Invocation is circuitous and indirect, like the flawed MapQuest directions

that have the driver stopping at a gas station anyway to get help.

No one wants to ask for help.

No one wants the magical formula to conjure up what can't be understood or tracked.

Which gets us back to invocation as
withholding.

*

As for withholding and invocation and delayed gratification—

this may seem a bit of a stretch—

some mythological texts suggest that in many cosmogonies a trope of "secretion" recurs.

The gods create worlds or other creatures by way of bodily secretion: spitting, shitting, weeping, bleeding.

What then are we to make of this in light of Freud's theory of anal retention?

Gaia held it in until she could hold it no more.

> (N.B. Virginia Woolf wrote in letter to a friend that she found the act of having a bowel movement pleasurably analogous to engaging in creative processes.)

The inevitable conclusion is that certain kinds of retentive

behaviors are also richly evocative, invocative.
The other conclusion is that we humans are made up of
divine waste.

*

Even with the use of magical formulas meant to invoke,
we, divine waste that we are,
can foresee so little.

Still, it should not come as any surprise, and in truth is entirely
predictable that having forced myself to shower before
commencing this poem, I slowly got dressed as I wrote it.

On January 1

for Norma Cole

Time is light,

that's all. Her tongue

a version, a map

version, where star maps

are always off-history whether

translating light

from a far galaxy or a local

starlet. "Oh!"

she said, a figure of herself,

"*Yes.*" Whereupon the light

threw itself down and pierced

her tongue, where it remained

like a stud, that she clicked against

her teeth as she spoke.

On Joy

Difficult to compass, joy.

Characterized by its leakage—
a hose pouring out onto hot pavement where
water pools, is absorbed, evaporates, but is
still cool underfoot.

Whipping cream poured into
bitter black tea as
a milky mushroom cloud forms.

The scent of used sheets being
peeled off the bed.

Joy's commitment to inconsistency,
to tardiness, to dust, litter, long
strands of fur on dark clothing.

The pure tone of the backyard chimes
when they collide
with an unsuspecting forehead.

The excess that is incidental,
unbidden, a tiny bit painful—
joy.

That which gives itself up, fully,
to the itch, scratching until
it draws blood and the itch

surrenders. Then
the illuminated red blot as it
clings to the skin
and hardens almost to blackness.

On Krakatoa

Time was a tumor in its very own landmass.

It couldn't have been more intrepid.

Think of the tumor speaking in first person:

    I climbed my own eruption.

    And higher.

    I said, "Excuse me" when I vomited.

Time was a contagion that forced currents against
their own grain.

    I projected my one, my central organ from the core of
    my body: that is, violently.

    That is, (intrepid) not the lung or heart, but the stomach.

Time was a countermeasure to civility: (Excuse me) infectious,
Time says

    I am the cancer

who ruptures the atmosphere with fumes of extraordinary beauty,

who climbs the sky with an affronting blush while the sun declines.

On the Last Supper

They often choose
pies.

Fried chicken and chicken fried steak,
sweet potatoes.

Two oranges and an orange-flavored drink: he had only
taken one bite before officers escorted him away.

But ice cream and milkshakes top the list

for the last meal. Mint
chip, chocolate.

In Texas, they've taken the last meal away.

One man wanted a single, unpitted, black
olive.

Canned spaghetti, not SpaghettiOs.

Pizza and ice cream, he shared with
his attorney.

Comfort food.

A 29,000-calorie meal. Unable to finish it.

Asked for pecan pie, but then said he'd
eat it later.

Or:
Not for me, but send
a veggie pizza to some homeless guy on the street.

Spinach, cooked apples, fries.

He had a very low I.Q. and it's now
widely accepted that he was innocent.

They executed him anyway. He
wanted ice cream. If they choose

dessert, they almost always
want some kind of ice cream.

On Light

Light, the well-meaning friend
who destroys a precious thing,
meaning only to caress it—

Laundry freshened in the warmth
of its gaze and bleached of color.
Withered petals. Melanoma.
The Great Salt Lake abolished to toxic dust.

Observer Effect:
what light witnesses, it
cannot help but change.

And yet light is the one loyalty.
What it eats it also feeds.

Light, struggling toward self-
awareness sheds itself in
lumens, footcandles, lightyears.

To know itself is to draw near and
draw back and draw near.

Light yearns like the heliotrope for light.

And so light
gulping

the loop of its throat
in the loop
of its throat finally

feasting on its own
equinoctial food.

On Love

"As the crow flies" suggests that flight is linear and direct.
But wings on air follow unpredictable currents.

Cliché mistakes destination for meaning.

And meaning is oblique.

The crow eats the seed as it finds it. Within the fires
of its gut, the seed's flesh is burned away.

Within the bowels
of the bird, fecal matter
gives the seed a hit of nitrogen.

Which is to say that love is an assignation
that accepts shit as enrichment.

The seed drops to the dirt wrapped in excrement.

It sprouts. Weedy, but weeds are hardy,

prickly, impervious to weather,
a growth fallen randomly into its inevitability.

On Men Named John

They all die.

John who spraypainted graffiti on a wall and told the judge
mournfully that he was just
trying to write a poem.

Of exposure.

John, although everyone,
even his dentist,
loved him.

Of despair.

John died in great old age, John
who endlessly attempted to
fix the leaking fountain.

It was fixed, it leaked, it was fixed, &c.

      That's almost a metaphor of eternity, John.

John who posted himself on an island
in a busy intersection, so

if the lights, the traffic, all of it
worked just right, you could
hand something off to him.

John, who is rumored to have died, but
since he got lost any place he ever tried to go,
how do we know?

John who may or may not be alive—we remember

him nonetheless,

his guileless kindness, his magic eagerness

to stop time for us.

On Misuse

Rubbed into the fissures of the thing is misuse.
Misuse as shellac.

Use, recast as something other than intended function.

Misuse, then, was so fragile and

smeared with promise. I promise.

I promised. Repeated applications of

promise deflect misuse with sheen. Its

very particular sheen that yellows, goes tacky with age.

A fingernail dug in comes out coated in a sticky residue,

having had no contact with the thing itself.

On Mortality

Fee   Fi   Fo   Fum

That is, a measure of four notes

Perfect 4/4 rhythm

No beat is to be accented over any other

One phrase; no rhyming rejoinder

Fee   Fi

on the invisible staff

Fo   Fum

Was it indeed a musical measure—

—a warning treble?   Fee

Fi

That it is human to syncopate, to subdivide

Fum   Fum   Fum

before infallible tone, the count entire, the melody neutral.

On Nightfall

The darkness reveals this

little nick

in the thumb knuckle,
a burden
to be carried on the back
of the hand.

Once

the dark
was a gesture, now

it blushes, tiny
incisions
of the descent, slits

of snow fingering

dusk.

On Nocturnal Light

Good darkness is its own address.

Flat. Darkness: flat

lying on top of the grooves of light.

Time's ritual, descant. How he

fits himself inside her and where

the good is in its riddle, now

the rite and rung hum. Snow

lofting up from its hillside. Bright

roil, wail for us. And warp this.

Rut in light. All,

almost, toward the inside air's inflowing it puzzles

to trace.

On Nourishment

Time's lozenge falls into a mouth.
Glands rise up and bathe it with spit.

The tongue, luminous and docile, absorbs
time as empty calories.

Time becomes
gummy as nougat, dissolving. Doesn't know

that it is digestible, that it has
made itself misty at the

border of the bloodstream. There

in the belly, time blossoms like an anemone.

A venous metronome, time
pulled from core to corpuscle,

where little sclerotic shards rise on

time's current. Time is circular,
a saline message—

An endless loop directs time
whose means are the ends it feeds itself.

On Numbness

Numbness, the neurological report says,
means damage.

Numbness: a blurred accent, a dialect spoken
by a person who cannot name her
country of origin.

A mouth clumsily forming vowels

around the bald patch of
unfeeling on the lips.

Left thumb disappeared,
fuzzy in the gesture that might clarify.

A velvety smear of sensation
down the right hip
and indistinct sparkling

like champagne

poured on the right foot.

Damage: a dulling slang drowns
out the voice of a person who
speaks pidgin anyway.

To her who assumes
this identity, a citizen

befuddled by destination,

it's not possible
to have arrived here from anywhere,

not possible to assimilate to new fluency.

On Only

Only stepped away from "if." Off the banks of the known world,

    into _____.

Only slept, and as it slept,

its particular world was altered.

Only to awaken unawares.

Only to change the idiom from "to fall asleep"

simply "to fall."

Only the surface.

An infinite series of reductions into

only what is left.

Only waking in the question.

Beneath the blanket.

Or, better—beneath the surface.

The breath in sleep, only how it alters as it wakes.

On the Outcome

Breath broken by the weight

of the voice.

All fall down

into the haven of

anxiety where all

can hide. The wasp leaves the windowsill.

The soft burr of its concern riding, again, the breath
of departure.

On Pages

Their purpose is to turn.

Literally,

against the clock.

The future, as read, is counterclockwise.

*

At last, alone or

singular,

the page measures its margin.

Creates the field, Janus-faced,

of the verso.

*

Time turns within its spine,

within its own signature, on itself.

*

Verso is to the clock as

signature is to time.

The page renounces itself in turning.

*

Turning on its own rhythm.

Within its own leaf:
(Seasonal. Deciduous. Falling.)

If time accretes as pages—

If it sheds itself—

*

A field on which to fall, fall backwards, forwards, fall

into the spine.

*

Time, two-faced on the page, doubles back

to the imaginary, sans body, field, or time. What part means
to whole,

spinning in the pivot of its own progress.

On Quim

Flooding the place the

body wants to believe

is

human   Shore

came all the way to sea   Water

The body

where solid and liquid

invert their

hollow

      asea   ashore

No   body

knows itself from

outside itself

Tide's fragrance   All

sense curling   inhuman

whose wet overflowed

the wave's comparison

On Rage

Rage is always past tense.

Wasn't that ridiculous.

Wasn't that inexplicable.

Cheerful music plays in the background,

as though it were playing right now.

As though you had gone into a yard in broad daylight
and picked flowers that

didn't belong to you.

What it means to say, the rage, is

what possession is. Possessed.

And after the fact, after the one moment,
the lucid storm of divine logic.

After the past tense.

The flowers are tucked into a vase and
sit on the table. Now they

are yours.

On Rape

You could tear the earring from your own ear.

You could lay a rumor on your tongue, then lick, lavish

it across skin.

You could change your pronoun from you to we or I.

They did.

I felt it inside me.

We could feel it and did. Did it.

We feel rupture from the inside whether

we come from inside or out.

Though technically nothing was broken, just

an orifice that wasn't part of us before, or

where you

are streaked and smeary, hurrying

past the anatomical, quickly

I was and

apprehended and you

cupped the cavity,

we held outside ourselves. I

a membrane and you

a surreptitious population,

as we are, a force that forgets,

that strikes their surface, ours,

after penetrating it, who, one might say,

was no pronoun at all, they or I

returning to that absence again

and over to prove it or you might

squeeze sweat from a crease,

pull hair from its follicle, whose smallest

vacancy, I

could justify you, they

say, you say—

could we prove again

were we

in or of, this who

prizes—that is, pries, open our own place

to insist who's always been inside it.

On Repetition

Have I

walked this route many times?

Have I imagined

what it means to lean

against?

Have I straightened my spine

against the curve it wants to make, where the

question makes

its own windy tune against the skin.

Have I got the melody fully within my head,

my literal head, not a mind, but bone

and hair and the tune

recirculating before it loops

toward the throat, intercepted

 by the tongue that pushes it forward—

was it pushed forward

of the mouth

through the lips

to be said (and not sung)

again?

Wasn't the obsession other

than a body? It was a chair

that one sat in, a chair another

tried to sit in as well. Wasn't the chair

rigid enough to pull

the clothing

off, to turn the

face to the table, a meal there,

one and the other, the

lips push forward—

food and furniture

rivals who wait

an arm's length away,

melody, like hair, tugged

to its protein, fed its

body to the place it

sat, this out-

of-reach structure.

Can a repetition interrupt itself?

Can a map be the repetition

of where a body has been?

Can the body perspire on the

basis of memory? A tune

embeds itself in muscle, hair,

tongue. Does

the gesture remember itself

as return, as repetition

even when the hands tug a different

shirt on or off?

The chair left a bruise on the leg,

didn't it, and by this the body repeats itself,

repeats the climbing back to

what it wants, to a structure

that is too rigid to hold it.

Doesn't the question repeat itself

just in being asked, even the first time? Does the shirt fit

as it peels away from torso, shoulders, arms? Didn't

they walk a long way, separately and

together? Is the chair a garment

the way a pair of pants is, that both

covers the body and so holds it together, and

does a lover also hold the body while

instead uncovering

it and in that way is a lover a chair? Did

they walk to the chair, did they climb

into it, did the

tune leave a little bruise on

the thigh?

Was memory a question that was liable

to betray?

Were they moving or holding, holding

nakedly, to the tune, a tune endlessly

subject to interruption?

Weren't they exhausted with their own

creaturely protein and bone, breath, tongue, and hum,

as it failed its own pattern?

Had they followed this route before, many

times before, they would have found themselves

also afterward, as they were, straining against the

furnishing that says a question is also a melody.

On [a theory of] Resolution

You attempt it when you are exhausted.

You tempt it.

What you refuse to do, you do. Do
it again. Undo. Do it, dote on it,

dare the thing to come back at you,

exhausted.

*

Aquinas said

that resolution is

a return to the source. But

how find one's way back

to what source? "Source,"

so called, does neither submit

nor supply itself. Aquinas

is dead. Neither here nor

gone. In your desk drawer,

you say, you have an envelope

that holds an old tooth, but when

opened: just enamel dust. Chalk.

Had the tooth a soul, you now see,

it has fled.

*

You were briefly not
a body, lifted
out of the body

then [pause] returned to
embodiment.

If only it was as easy as death,
only death,

[pause]
only one shoulder
scrunching up in pain,

lopsided as death, and the body's
final return to it.

*

The theory is a body after all,

after all the body is
its center:

the navel.

And all else.

All else is extra, extraneous,

extruded

like the aorta whose
heart is not a compass, whose
feathery extra

artery is inexact, a needle
excised from

direction. The theory

is resolute and compassing, so earnest
as to be
inexact, as to
lose its way home.

*

Throughout its life,
the theory's

toenails grow, growling

in their flesh beds. Growing
in the coil

and ingrown. Coil or curl.
Theory is this protein, and

resolution is the rind, the
rounding curve of what it cannot be.
Ingrown.

So the flesh rejects its product. So
the projection loves itself warping,

forcing itself into its source.

Similarly, the mouth alludes to
the hinge of the jaw. Example: jaw snapping
to closure and lips'

stretchy allusion to
acute angle.

The mouth uttering words
against or astray
the bone that would be
its base, its basis. But

a mouth only borrows the bone
of the jaw. Mouth ajar.

Pursed and lisped. Contraction
of the lips. O.

The mouth has no source and returns
to its periphery. And so it speaks,
circular, bereft of resolution. O.

O wrinkling around what it has no basis for saying.

*

Resolution resolves its theory
thinking again of body.

Resolution's lesser-known organs,
each in their own time. Timid,

perhaps. Example: nipple contracting
to the mouth on an infant.

Trace of milk transacting
what no one will witness:

the source as it feeds, leaving itself.

Taken by the mouth, and the mouth
incapacitated from utterance

by hunger.

                        *

You find you are so tired. You find
the very weave of your skin

so tired it tears.

You observe tears
gliding down your face. You
and only you

are these fluids, these rips,
this tear in its ripeness

dripping onto the wound
which also flows

with its own flow. You lick
blood, salty as

snot and a tear also
finds its way

casually

into your mouth.

*

That is: not resolution, but resignation.
That is: proof that Aquinas was correct.

That blood is commanded
by its central organ you call heart,

to leave the center, to heave
toward extremity

and then to return.

The circulatory system
is apparently theological.

Heart, headstrong, admits
to the body

that it is the source, and all
sources are

pumps pumping. Go away.
Come back. Resigned,

no more than that,

to some form of infinity.

*

Refutation:

You cut your hair.

You cut your nails.

You hiss spit from your lips.

You are entitled, even,

to lose a limb or two should

circumstances require.

At times, you go away and do not return to

yourself.

You may weep into this brutal tiredness if you
wish.

*

As you dream at night, you do

dream of swallowing.

Merely your own saliva.

You dream you are

awake, you dream

the fine silken fluid

in your throat arose

beneath your tongue.

You dream you have swallowed

this much, and no more, not

that it tastes so piquant, particular,

or sweet as its tide rises

within you and resumes

to its source as you swallow.

You dream you have

swallowed because you

are thirsty and only thirsty.

*

Yet

in some bodily occult,

nothing is swallowed.

While the body, why, it

remains aligned to its

thirst. You know this.

You deny this. The theory

of resolution is meteorological
and not eternal. All resolves

to a hot day, the self scorched

to its limit. In humid crease

beneath the breast, borne

in the bend of the elbow, armpit,

your body sends itself forth as sweat

then quietly resorbs to the source,

at least the skin of the source, at least

a salty residue says: something has

resolved itself and is gone.

On Sadness

One needs a means of storage for the surplus.

Containers for the dry goods.

Bottles for the liquid.

It alters as it collects. A scuff of mold on the grain.

Fluids fermenting.

On Self Care

Self-abased, self-contempt, self-same the

injunction to self cure that self's

supervisor delivers to the subordinate

self.

How does the self massage the self, sleep

the self in, feed the self pancakes, select

the self's bouquet from something other

than the detritus of the grocery store's

stock?

What little rivulet carved out of the obdurate day

might somehow become a vast Grand Canyon of

the self's self-adoration?

The self has skepticism to which no
self can answer.

The self lessens itself to the supervisor's

lesson. To take care. To take care of a self

straitened by design to the constraints

of the lesson. Be a self so condensed

to the lesson's condescension.

On Snow

Things fall

hesitantly, differently,

unsure of their season.

*

If the conditions

had a melody,

they would be half-aware, humming it over and over:

minor key, then major, then minor.

The world, then, is only a world inside

its own weather,

a diffident

fleck, the tune

*

worn or melted, eroded into a key

that rhymes indeterminately.

*

If melody had

a memory, would

it be white
and discordant, oblivious of

gravity,
afraid?

*

Snow's attempt to rhyme with conditions

of atmosphere. Snowflake's

melting asymmetry,

the uneven simile of relation

undoes itself.

*

Off-key

rhyme—winter's

barbed delicacy

undoes itself by falling to

what it hoped was a prior circumstance,

lopsided season.

On the Difference Between "Speculum," "Speculate," and "Spectate"

A duck-billed device

used to see into a hollow

of a body.

Of the body.

*

He splashed cold fluid on my vagina, repeating,
"I bet you're just hating me right now, just hating me"

and then he opened the speculum.

*

Meaning: instrument for rendering

a part accessible to observation.

From the root, "spek": to observe

Root found also in

despicable
suspicion
spy

*

She,

once a midwife,

says, "It

is like twins in the womb. One

of them doesn't want to leave—'*It*

will be the end of us'—

and the other says they '*must*

go.' They don't know they

are about to be born." But

what she's talking about is death,

not birth.

*

In other words, we speculate,

the cavity is full and finds

its meaning in emptying

itself.

*

If the orifice is not a cavity
but a habitation.

Speculate on who inhabits, who
is habitation.

The orifice of time and geography heavy
with law,

and each pocket swelling

(as regulated)

to hold more.

*

How many times have I had the speculum
inserted and opened

after which the practitioner
left the room, left
me there.

"Sorry, I had to take that call."
"Sorry for that interruption."

But to be opened shouldn't mean
to be interrupted. Speculation

stretches past comfort

into conjecture.

One practitioner finally returned
with a mirror, saying,

"I thought you might want to take a look."

On the Steadfast

It did not go away. It failed, ever,

to part from itself.

It bared its skin to sunlight and ate

vitamin D.

Back of itself, it knew the secrets; it melted

the prick of bitterness beneath its tongue.

*

You did not trust what you know.

Felt its hands, its hand, on your breasts.

All the other lovers the steadfast purported

to love were equally steadfast. To

whom

does loyalty return, like

sunlight burning through overcast.

Too much of a good thing

we will never know.

*

You

or we

hear the bell ring the hour.

And then

it rings again. In case. To reassure.

That time is genuine

time. Steadfast as it passes.

Rings each hour twice.

Lover a bit late. The gap in the phrase

that falls short of a sentence is a sentence.

Reassure us.

*

The steadfast in broad daylight.

The steadfast tangled in pronouns.

What we no longer wanted.

We thought.

Grief at betrayal

mingled.

The legs striding through noon, ripe

with contempt

at the solid ground beneath,

absorbing sunlight.

                                        *

Not reassure. Prove

that a day is 24 hours. Emits

and then sucks back itself.

Repeats.

The steadfast squints in the glare, shifts

the bitter nub beneath its tongue before it dissolves.

*

The steadfast was less than kind

because such things do burn. Time, that is,

compelled to perform its duties.

The sun at the apex of the sky.

Noon was a sentence from which subject and verb

drooped, dropped off.

Some part will come back or part

from itself. Naked, it absorbed nutriment from its atmosphere.

Ever. Failsafe. Burned from the root of the tongue

up to the climax overhead.

On Surviving

Unforgettable, the man in the suit who seized
her five-year-old body and pulled it onto his lap.

The bright dusk of leaping up and getting away.

*

How many bodies
have wrestled that light, how

many secrets apprehended, then
hidden.

Light was this parade, this lost history,
a procession of avid hands
invading the body, a shimmy,

—shock that cannot be unshocked,

blouse torn inside out by the, by the,
the fading light of once more getting away.

There are caches of this radiance
inside each woman,
hoarded.

*

Walking in darkness she cannot unrecollect—
how not remember—

the man who thought it was a good joke
to jump from the edges. *Boo.*

And the lit circle of her hands
around his throat.

On Terseness

Here's how I interrupted my story.

How I burnt my fingers on a match.

Here's how I scared the bears away from the garbage.

Underneath the great deluge there was nothing much.

It soaked up all that it could (story, fire, wild beast) but most of it

is excess, is not beholden to absorption, has fled within the bulk of itself.

On Tolerance

Tolerance closed its eyes and the world lost gravity.

The brain revolved inside the cranium, like a compass.

But then gave way.

Yes, it did float.

It floated within its past tense and its past tenselessness.

This buoyancy called itself endurance, endurance

functioning more as a medium. It was

the lawn chair tethered to the helium balloon that ascended.

On Trust

One trusts that a mockingbird
is a bird

and that it can imitate
what it is not.

One trusts that a sentence is a complete thought.

One invents rational ways
to practice this
irrational, irritation, ration.

Trust is a stutter fraying the complete thought,

belief released from creed.

One musters confidence, walking in the dark

as the mockingbird trusts only its own
voice as it trills: frog, crying baby,
an oration of receding siren.

On Truth

Truth is a freeway, no, *the* freeway,
definite article,

design for efficient conveyance.

Seen overhead, truth's overlapping ramps, curves
sexy as a bullwhip.

Truth slides into traffic.

[Sigalert: defined by California State Patrol as "any unplanned
event that causes the closing of one lane of traffic for
30 minutes or more"]

Midnight drunk swerving between lanes. Encampment
in the depression between highways.

Shorthand: 5, 22, 80, 580, 880, 101, 405, 605. Code,
as in "Take the 405 to the 110 to 5." Breathe deep

below the inversion layer.

The truth is,
Jesus saves. And Sweet James
offers justice: 1-800-881-2021. Another client protected.

Cut off by an asshole, unavoidable mound of
truth dislodged directly ahead. Verity and its variants.

Interminable wait, dead stop,

a glance into the rearview mirror seconds
before the collision.

A vantage from which to see and be consumed
by wildfire. A mirage of ice plant and palm trees

by which we are beguiled as we swarm forward.

On Typos

"Homer was a blind poet who resighted poetry."

In the woodland you were

dear and deer.

I might almost have said it simultaneously.

Where your

who are

you're

would land. Uncorrectable and

I might have said there

all at once

where

they're grazing

among wares, air and err

It's these,

a thesis:

where made

to *wear* its self, it's

tangled in samenesses—a little

grove of the subtlest confusions and

a tune

I might have sung. A site wrung of

these is

a rung of sight
cited

synchronous. At once attunement

dear and recited unseeing. Whose words

might be there and theirs.

On Unconsciousness

in memory of Bill Bennett

There are some events which one wishes would never end,
and some

for which the word event makes little sense.

> Separately, the mind views a demonstration of itself
> straining to uphold

a complex melody.

Abruptly, it is not a mind anymore.

The event, having flowered, spread itself beyond its own
boundaries.

One wonders whether the demonstration will be able to wake
itself up later, if

it will feel inclined to loll in the flower, the flowers,
the ravishment of its own

extending success, a display

of little sense, yet musical. Such that it holds up its instrument,
wavering

before it topples into inversion, melodic complexity,

irresistible occasion, this

garland of demonstrations.

On Understanding

in memory of Anselm Hollo

The lines in the drawing are not straight. Their

crookedness proves something lingers

behind the exterior.

Exterior on which snow and daylight fall with equal authority.

Nothing can remediate this basic helplessness.

The dying man is angry, "They told me I could get better."

Curses.

He lies naked on the surface of his death,
covered by moving air.

One does not apprehend—grasp—this vast flatness.
The way it purports to be

landscape and always also behind

landscape.   Not that one wishes

to lie atop it, cool and bare.   But

to surmise that beneath, if one could find beneath, there

would be a passing warmth buckling the plane.

On My Valentine

It died, for instance, of neglect and was

replicated itself.

From a distance, it moved like

an animal. Up close, it drank

what it was given.

Flowering, furred foot. This creature—

stay

—wavers between its self, self-canceling

like thirst and the drought

it takes in, eases.

Another Variant on Vision

See, the voyeur says, though only

to herself: knotty. You watch. You tie together a series
of knots so

continuous that you make a braid.

On the Vote

This is the artwork of effort.

Poll tax. A festoon of chads hung

from the mantle

of justice. Yet still

a dearth of ballots. The longest line

drawn

across precinct and day

and through our

names. We are all

felons. Denial makes

us thirsty. No one

may bring us water

as we wait. A performance

whose rhythm is obstruction.

A gallery

of empty voting stalls.

The dead, they claim,

vote and vote and vote.

We hear their chorus. We

tally our attempts as

a lost art.

On Walking in the San Andreas Fault

Walking is the only consolation

where the very soil is contaminated with instability,

where the soothing maternal voice of reason doesn't say "There, there," but

"Where, where."

> The sky above threatens perennially to fold and drop
> temblor, seismism, tremor.

Best to take shelter in the fault. Better to walk on friction itself, heels in the

where-where, treading on that soothing voice

because it is

a fount, a full breast so ready to

release the foremilk of solace.

Walking is a consolation that
hardly worries the nursling gap in

the world which suffers from its own mild
infinite, where

reliance and need, where. Maternal

fault. One hesitates to use the word "cradle."

Heels pummel the udder, rut, croon of rift.

On Xs as Kisses
[On Addenda]

What she pulled from

her nostril: a slick sash

that she draped around her

shoulders in celebration of

graduation, a smart

tiara, a spun-sugar

confection.

There was no erratum, the

addenda were like shining

Xs at the end of the letter: could

be kisses or

extinction.

The margin that she drew

from herself as sheen, a lacquer

of surface, no erratum amid the imperative of

inside-out. She draws forth the sepia speech scroll

that marks her surplus.

On "X equals"

One long, ongoing phrase that tucks in
its many false starts until the contradictions
lay lip to lip and decide not to self-cancel as
the film of sweat crystallized its
own salt and the moving limbs took on
a sheen, button pushed back and forth through
its hole, stutter or, better, sleeptalk, not
backwards in time but two
incisions, made diagonally, and the skin
magically puckers for they were no edges, they
were lips, arms flexed before the body, the lacings
of the shoes crossed, and loosening and as long as
grammar had seemed hopeful, the sentence
had transubstantiated into words—lapses in
order were not lapses in flow but the erotic
pink of the scar, whose healing was a tangle in every
instance, in every recurring loss of the grain
of salt to the tongue, a securing two stitches whose
X models intersection over breach, movement
where nothing is equal, almost invisible wound cut
uncut to rhythm.

On Youth

Narrative makes a fat circle. Those who know it

also know its Grand Tour. Here
where adolescents pick at their acne, buy souvenirs, sleep
their way into maturity.

The circuit of the traveler, as with the globe
tout court
is a pattern known as the equator.

They sing songs, ditties, sneezing as they go.

As they go, they know
their itinerary by its accessories:
equator, equation, equate, equable.

They surrender to these equivocations.

The young travel into this most intense sunlight by
having faith.

I mean to say our youth
bring the loop to completion

by inhaling through their mouths. I mean to say they

can carry a tune without necessarily singing it. They, they, they:

how our company travels, swaddled in the tour bus,

as passive as the lost child who

abandons herself to endless hiccupping.

On Zero

O, as in exclamation.   O.

O. Zero as acknowledgement. Oh. I see.

O's apostrophe. A hole in the world. Not aperture. O,

for it is to you I speak, O, you.

ROOF BOOKS
the best in language since 1976

Recent & Selected Titles

Roof Books are distributed by
SMALL PRESS DISTRIBUTION
1341 Seventh Street • Berkeley, CA. 94710-1403.
spdbooks.org

Roof Books are published by
Segue Foundation
300 Bowery #2 • New York, NY 10012
seguefoundation.com